CW00373443

Games to Play with Your Cat

Paul Berman and Roger Markman

Illustrations by Steve Ridgway

Published by Sigma Leisure – an imprint of
Sigma Press, 1 South Oak Lane, Wilmslow, Cheshire SK9 6AR, England.

British Library Cataloguing in Publication Data
A CIP record for this book is available from the British Library.

ISBN: 1-85058-798-1

Typesetting and Design by: Sigma Press, Wilmslow, Cheshire.

Cover Design: Sigma Leisure

Printed by: MFP Design & Print

Contents

Introduction

This book came about as a result of a number of conversations. We both have pet cats and got talking about the sorts of games we played with them. In talking to other cat owners we learned that many of them also had favourite games that their cats liked. There are lots of books available which tell you how to choose a cat and look after him (or her – throughout this book, we use 'him' just to save space) but we couldn't find a book which described actual games that you can play with your cat. We then spoke to a lot of people, tried out a lot of games, and put the best ones in this book.

Every cat has his own personality and will respond in different ways to different stimuli, but we hope that your cat will enjoy trying out the various games and will find their particular favourites. We've also included some background information on cat behaviour which may help you to understand why your cat plays in the way that he does. We offer our grateful thanks to Helen Whitehead for her expert help in preparing these sections. We hope that you enjoy reading the book and, most of all, enjoy playing with your cat.

All the illustrations in the book are the work of Steve Ridgway. Steve has been an artist for many years, and his speciality is scraperboard work. The scraperboard itself is a piece of stiff board covered in a thin layer of fine white clay. Some scraperboards come already coated in black ink, which can then be carefully scratched away, leaving the white clay showing through. With white board, Steve uses a fine paintbrush to draw a kind of silhouette of the picture in black ink, and then puts in the detail by scraping away the ink with a sharp craft knife to leave the white parts. That's really all there is to it, but it takes a lot of practice and talent to get up to a professional standard! The scraperboard medium is especially suitable for cat pictures, because you can either draw each strand of fur separately for a vivid portrait, or else use a softer touch to give a fluffy effect.

Steve drew all the cats in this book from photographs – we took lots of photographs of our own cats and friends' cats playing the games in the book and then Steve used the best ones for reference. You can contact Steve on steve_ridgway@hotmail.com if you'd like to commission an original portrait of your cat from him.

- Paul Berman and Roger Markman

The authors' cats

Hi, my name is Cleo! I've lived with Roger since 1997, when I was very young. As well as my 'official' bed, I often sleep on Roger's study chair in front of the computer. I like to sleep about sixteen hours a day, but not usually all at once. My favourite games are 'stairball' and 'fishing line'. Sometimes I play hide and seek with Roger, and it always surprises me how easy it is to fool him into thinking I'm in one place when I'm in another. My favourite foods are chicken and crunchy cat biscuits. I quite like watching the animal programmes on TV. I can come and go whenever I want, which is great because I've got lots of friends I visit, both human and feline.

I've told Roger that this book is a good idea because not enough humans play with us cats, and that's a pity because we love to play and generally scamper about. I like living with Roger because he plays with me and listens to what I say. I'm sure he can understand nearly every word, although my cat friends say it's probably my tone of voice he's picking up on. I reckon in a few years I'll have trained him perfectly!

I'm Twirl, though I'm usually known as Woolly or The Woolly Pet. I'm quite old now, in my middle teens, but I can still chase things in the garden as fast as ever, though I'm not quite as good at jumping as I was once. I've lived with Paul since I was a kitten, and I have to say that he's a pretty good owner – he feeds me on demand and he'll always get out of his chair to open the front door for me when I want to go out. I particularly like playing any kind of ball games. My second favourites are fishing line games because I like to lurk behind the furniture and watch what's going on anyway – and if there's a game in it, so much the better!

I stay indoors a lot more now

than when I was a kitten, but I still like to get out when the weather's warm and dry – there are lots of sheltered places in the garden where I can curl up and go to sleep. I purr a lot – but what cat wouldn't, with all that nice food, good company and lots of play? Not a bad life really.

Tube Ball

All you need for this game is a table tennis ball and a cardboard tube. The sort of tube used inside rolls of bathroom tissue or kitchen paper is ideal. Table tennis balls are perfect for this game – they're light so they cannot hurt the cat if they drop on his nose, and they also make a distinctive noise when they bounce on a hard surface.

The best way to start playing, particularly if your cat has never played Tube Ball before, is to drop the ball through the tube a few times to show your cat what happens. When you've got his attention, hold the ball just above the top of the tube and then let it drop through the tube. In your first few sessions playing this game, your cat should at least watch it falling out of the bottom of the tube and, with luck, he'll want to bat it with his paw as it falls. He'll have more time to hit the ball if you hold the tube further above the ground. To vary the game, sometimes you can pretend to drop the ball through the tube but actually hide the ball in your hand at the last moment, or you can drop the ball into the tube but stop it falling through by putting your finger under the bottom of the tube.

Other variations include tilting the tube as the ball goes through it so that the ball runs off to one side. When the cat has got used to chasing the ball when it falls through, you can stand the tube on the ground and drop the ball in, so that your cat has to get the ball out from inside the tube. For really advanced players, you can use two tubes and hold them in your hand with the tops together and the bottoms angled apart. This time, when you drop the ball, the cat won't know which tube the ball's going to drop out of. Alternatively, use just one tube but more than one ball. Move the tube about slightly as you drop the balls through, and then your cat will be in paradise with balls everywhere.

It's always good to tidy up after yourself – I know because my mother told me (even if I don't always actually do it). My friend Mary learned this lesson the hard way after she had been playing tube ball with her cat Mr Paws, and she forgot to put everything away again. Long after the household had gone to sleep, Mr Paws decided to make one of his routine inspections of the house. He particularly inspects the kitchen floor in case there are any tasty scraps of food which haven't been thrown away. On this occasion, he found the table tennis ball in the hall, where they'd been playing Tube Ball, and seized the opportunity to practise his footballing skills. Table tennis balls may sound pretty quiet when there's lots of other noise around, but in the dead of night and on a wooden floor, they sound more like the army attacking. After learning this useful if tiring lesson, Mary got into the routine of putting all the cat's toys away at bedtime.

When they first started playing this game, it took Mr Paws a few sessions to get into Tube Ball, but now it's one of his favourite games. It also has the advantage that once he's played it with Mary a few times, he's quite happy to chase the ball around the room until it's time to go to sleep again.

– RM

Curiosity

Curiosity is said to kill the cat, but on the whole, the insatiable curiosity that intrepid kittens show about the world is beneficial. The constant exploration of its environment, together with wise words from mum, teaches a kitten all it needs to know.

As they are by nature solitary hunters in the wild, cats need to learn all the necessary survival skills in the very first few months of their life before going off to fend for themselves. Pack animals, such as dogs and humans, are not on their own at a young age – they have back-up and access to advice, and so the drive to learn fast may be less intense. Investigating new objects is part of the play repertoire of all kittens, and many cats retain this joy in novelty into their adulthood and even into old age. Introducing new games, or putting a favourite game aside for a time to bring it out afresh later, keeps our pets' minds and bodies active and alert.

Cats in the wild usually hunt small, fast-moving prey and therefore games that involve smallish quick-moving objects are usually very popular with household pets. The types of prey that cats chase often run in spurts rather than in a continuous sprint and will twist and turn to maximise their chances of escape. Playthings that can be made to imitate this type of action will excite their curiosity and be firm favourites with most cats. Another prey escape strategy that can be imitated with toys to attract and keep cats' attention is that of freezing into absolute stillness. Anything that moves quickly and then suddenly stops will provoke an intense scrutiny and a tentative tap from an outstretched paw to check how awake the prey (toy) is.

Boxes are a firm favourite of the curious cat. Any size of box will do, but boxes that are just too small to hold the cat seem to be best, apart from that most attractive box sitting outside the house, the family car. While not usually liking to travel far in it, cats like playing in and around this extension of the house that smells like home but with extra car-specific smells. We need to be careful though. One person I heard of had to have their car taken apart piece by piece as their kitten had found his way into an inaccessible place deep inside their car's interior – so be warned. It may be safer to postpone using the car adventure playground until the curious kitten is too big to fit into small openings.

9

Flashlight

The idea for this game came to me one winter's evening when the curtains had not been drawn in the living room and the light from the street lamp shone in brightly through the window. The wind was agitating the large old oak tree which stands in front of the house and it made a shadow-play of light patterns which danced across the living room carpet. Cleo, my cat, was drawn like a magnet to this flickering effect and began pouncing with glee on the spots of light and dark. Aha! The seed of an idea was sown.

To play flashlight, any ordinary flashlight will do, but the more powerful the better. Start by showing it to your cat and switching it on and off. Next, shine a circle of light directly onto the floor in front of you for a couple of seconds. This should really interest your cat, who will start to puzzle over where the light has come from. Next, start to move the spot of light from side to side slowly, keeping well within the immediate area of your cat's focus. At this point, he may well start to pounce and generally hunt the spot of light.

This basic game can be extended and expanded. If the flashlight is powerful enough, try shining it at a greater distance, such as from upstairs to downstairs, or from one room to another. As with the basic game, the technique is to shine the light for bursts of 10 to 15 seconds and to move it relatively slowly within your cat's immediate vision. This will make it less likely that he will ignore the light because it is too difficult to track and hunt.

One development of the game makes use of two or more flashlights. To play this version of the game, start by shining the two spots of light close together as if they were one light. Then start to make the two pools of light move away from each other, and watch to see what your cat does next. This can be utterly fascinating and is a great stimulus to the development of your cat's thinking and decision-making powers. In nature, this would be like deciding 'shall I pounce on mouse A or mouse B?'

There is also the shadow version of the game. To play this, you need to make some very simple paper cut-outs of shapes such as stars, butterflies, birds and similar. Shine the light onto a suitable wall while holding the paper cut-out in front of the light so as to cast a shadow. Dangling the cut-out from a fine thread stops the shadow of your hand from showing as well, and makes the shadow shape even more mysterious. Move the light and the cut-out about, and occasionally turn the light off and on again to make a really effective and exciting wall shadow display which your cat will love to hunt.

This is only a very simple introduction to light-play games. Yet more variations are possible with coloured filters, mirrors and more complex arrangements of lights. The only limitation is your imagination. Buy a set of rechargeable batteries – you'll be using your flashlight a lot.

Going back to the inspiration for the flashlight game – the light from the street lamp shining through the tree – when I play flashlight at night with my house lights out, I always draw the curtains tight. The sight of someone going round a darkened house, shining a torch here and there, would surely make a watchful neighbour summon the police to come and catch the burglar.

– RM

13

Skin Deep

One of the most delightful parts of a cat is its beautiful soft furry coat. The range of colours, patterns and length of hair is enormous, and every one has its devotees. A cat's skin is more loosely attached to the underlying surface than is human skin, and this probably helps with flexibility and suppleness, and helps decrease the severity of any fighting wounds. The coat itself is usually double-layered, with a layer of soft short hairs next to the skin to help with thermal insulation. On top of them are the longer, stronger hairs that carry the colour and pattern. In some cats, the colours of the two coats are quite similar and you don't really notice that the coat is not completely uniform. My neighbours had a cat called Rupert, now playing in cat heaven, who had a white undercoat and a black topcoat, so that you could run your finger along his fur, against the natural direction of the coat, and make a distinct groove of white against the black background.

Intensive breeding programmes have produced extremes of styles with, for instance, long undercoats and topcoats in the Persian cat, and only the short undercoat in the Cornish Rex. To keep their coats in good condition, cats indulge in grooming activities for up to half their waking hours. We are not talking about the quick paw-lick that a cat does to divert attention away from a momentary loss of dignity or to relieve tension, but the full wash and brush up.

Thanks to their famous suppleness, cats can lick and clean virtually every part of their bodies. Very long-haired cats, especially Persians, will usually need help in keeping their coats clean and free of tangles, and a daily combing will be a pleasure for both owner and pet (but be gentle with the comb if there are any tangles). Regular, thorough grooming also keeps down the flea burden carried by a cat, though modern anti-flea treatments are probably the best solution if total freedom from fleas is wanted. A cat's tongue is ideally suited to the task of grooming. There are backward-facing hooked structures on the top of the tongue which act like a comb when grooming. The saliva a cat uses when washing has been identified as a possible reason for the allergic reaction some people have to cats. Watching a family pet groom itself is a fine way to pass the time – joining in is even better.

15

Fishing Line – Version 1

Fishing lines of various types are probably the most popular sort of cat toys seen in pet shops. There are many different games that can be played with them, and they are a must for all playful cat owners. It is very easy to make one of these cat toys yourself, and if you make your own it will be tailored to your exact requirements and will also be very robust and long lasting. The cost of making your own fishing line is very small.

The actual 'rod' can be any type of wooden or plastic stick, but I favour a length of garden cane. These canes can be bought very cheaply from any garden centre. The 'line' is best made from a length of strong cord or string. I use nylon picture cord myself, as I have a large roll of it at home. You need to cut a length of cord about a metre and a half long and attach it to the thin end of the rod. Simply tie the cord to the rod and wrap some adhesive tape around the knot to make it neater and more secure. Any kind of adhesive tape will do.

Finally, it's a matter of attaching your choice of toy to the end of the line. Whatever toy you choose, just tie it onto the end of the cord. Then you can change the toy any time you like to give your games a bit more variety. Likely toys you can use include a toy mouse, a ball (including the types that make a noise), a butterfly and so on. You can make a butterfly by cutting out a square of coloured cloth and tying it in the middle, which instantly makes a butterfly shape. Really, any kind of small toy can be tied to the end of your fishing line, and it's only a matter of imagination as to what you can use.

Using your completed fishing line, you can simulate the movements of the various kinds of prey which your cat would hunt in nature. For 'flying' prey, you'll need some 'perches' such as kitchen chairs, stair treads, the tops of boxes and so on. Make sure that all the perches onto which your cat might jump are strong enough.

Holding the rod in your hand, make the toy take off and fly from one perch to another, skimming the ground in between perches. Your cat should show great interest in this. I made a fishing line for my friend Mary and her cat Elvis, who becomes very excited (all shook up) when they start playing this game. Vary the flight to include hovering over the perch for a few seconds. You can also try overflying the cat itself, with the toy at different heights above the cat's head. With so many different styles of flying, varying the height, speed and direction, you can make this an infinitely varied and fascinating game for you and your cat. You can also vary the degree of enthusiasm to suit the age and energy level of your own cat. Elvis is not as young as he used to be, so Mary plays the game with slower swooping and shorter hopping of the toy.

Don't forget that your cat must be allowed to win in the end and have the fun of catching the flying target. If the target toy gets chewed up and destroyed, just make another one and you're in business again. Whenever Elvis destroys his toy, Mary gives me back the cane ('Return to Sender' …) and I fit a new toy for him.

– RM

For another 'Fishing Line' game, see page 58 …

17

"*It always darts out of the way — just when I'm going to catch it.*"

19

Cat Vision

The cat and its human (we're not really owners) in some ways see the world in the same way. We both have forward-pointing eyes at the front of our faces, which give good stereoscopic vision and help us to calculate the position and distance of objects very accurately. Having said that, in most other respects a cat's and a human's vision differ considerably, as you would expect when cats are nocturnal hunting carnivores and humans are diurnal hunter/gatherers.

Relative to its skull size, a cat's eye is huge, as are the eyes of other nocturnal creatures. It is not true that a cat can see in complete darkness, but it is much better than us at seeing in very low levels of light. The lens of the eye is set back in the eyeball and the pupil can open very wide in low light, giving the cat's eye very good light-gathering ability. Having collected the maximum amount of light available, the cat has another trick up its sleeve, or rather behind its retina. The retina – the layer at the back of the eye which contains special cells called cones which react to colours, and rods which detect shades of black and white – receives the light and passes the message of what it detects in the way of colour and shade to the brain. In the cat, behind the retina is the tapetum, a mirror-like surface which reflects back the light that missed the rods and cones the first time, giving the receptor cells a second chance. It is the tapetum which gives a cat's eye that beautiful glow so often seen in photographs – so much prettier than the red-eye effect one often gets when photographing one's nearest and dearest humans.

There has often been discussion about whether cats see colour or not. As they do have cones for colour, it would seem that they should be able to, and experiments have now shown that they can distinguish between colours such as red and green. It appears that colour vision is not important to cats. As with humans, in low levels of light at night, everything appears in shades of black and white and an appreciation of colour is not necessary for survival.

What visual stimuli grab the attention of your cat? Slow-moving things are often ignored by pusskin, but a fast or jerkily-moving object will catch the eye of most cats and prove irresistible. Many of our games in this book use quick movements to get the cat's attention. The majority of programmes on television are of no interest to cats, the exceptions being the special videos of quick-moving and colourful fish that have been produced. On the other hand, a cat I know called Raksha (half moggie, half champion Persian) loved watching the skiing, particularly the giant slalom and the ski jumping. Every Sunday she would sit down with her human and spend a happy hour being entertained by these curious humans on sticks.

Dominoes

Do you like watching those spectacular displays of millions of dominoes knocking each other over which you see from time to time on TV? Well, here is a way of doing something along those lines at home with your own cat. This game is best suited to the more adventurous cat who's not put off by a bit of noise.

To play this game you need a set of dominoes, which are readily available from most toy shops if you don't already have any. You play this game with your cat ideally on the floor, not on the table. You can begin by setting up a very simple upside-down 'U' shape from three dominoes. Show this to your cat and demonstrate knocking it over. From this simple beginning, you can go on to build more elaborate structures.

Things you might like to try include 'Stonehenge' – a circle of upside-down 'U's all linked together. Another variation along these lines, like a smaller version of the world-record domino-toppling feats, is a circle of dominoes standing on their short edges so that if any one is knocked over, a 'chain reaction' results and they all come toppling down in a very spectacular fashion. Yet another alternative is the pyramid, made by building a three-sided base of about four to six vertical dominoes per side, topped by domino lintels and then another storey on top if you've got a steady hand. As a variation on the same theme, lay two dominoes parallel, side by side, about half their length apart. Next, lay two more dominoes crossways on top to make a square shape. Continue building until you have a tower a few storeys high. This structure should be quite stable and will require determined biffing by your cat to demolish it.

My own cat Cleo loves playing dominoes. One interesting thing she sometimes does is to attempt to pull the spots off the dominoes. If you find that your cat is attracted to the spots, sort out the dominoes with most spots on and use those. You can then try mixing in the occasional lesser-spotted dominoes to see the results. In a similar way to the 'Spinner Winner' game in this book, you can use the dominoes to let your cat find the winning numbers. Make a note of the numbers he chooses by watching how he paws at the different dominoes.

My friend Aysha has a cat which loves to play with dominoes which she keeps in an old metal biscuit tin. All she does is to put the tin on the floor with the lid off and Snoopy does the rest. He reaches in with his paw and bats the dominoes around, making lots of noise. Sometimes he flicks a domino out of the tin and then chases it around the floor. In this case, Snoopy is clearly attracted to the rattling sounds that the dominoes make against the metal walls of the tin, and the noise of a domino sliding across the floor and colliding with the furniture and the walls. The domino tin is one of the few confined spaces that Snoopy doesn't actually want to get into to have a quick sleep. I think it's the colder metal surface which is less nest-like than his favourite cardboard box.

All in all, dominoes can provide hours of fun for you and your cat, and they last forever. They challenge the owner's imagination to invent new ways of using them – here we have shown only a small selection of possible games using these fascinating little black blocks which have been around for centuries.

– RM

*"I was a
bit startled
by the clatter
they made
when they
fell down."*

25

Smell and Taste

Humans have a relatively poor sense of smell. We can distinguish between good and rotten food, and a perfumed rose smells quite different from its neighbouring cowpat, but most of us do not rely on smell to navigate our way around. The cat, in contrast, has a highly-developed sense of smell that can distinguish minute differences in apparently extremely similar scents. We can all tell if an un-neutered tomcat has visited the area and sprayed urine around, but the cat of the house can discern whether the visiting cat is known to them or is a stranger. To facilitate this remarkable talent, the cat's nose is full of thin layers of bone covered with mucous membrane (called olfactory epithelium) which is sensitive to odour. This gives the cat about twice as much scent-sensitive area as a human has.

The cat uses this sense to interpret markings left by other cats, and to 'try out' food before he decides to eat it. Cats, like some other mammals including hamsters, have an extra scent organ. This is the Jacobson's or vomeronasal organ. It consists of two sacs that open into the mouth behind the incisor teeth. To use this organ, a cat pulls back its upper lip and opens its mouth slightly, drawing air into the sacs.

It seems that this sense is partly smell and partly taste. The cat appears to use this mouth action, called 'Flehmen', to judge the receptiveness of cats of the opposite sex. A cat who loses his sense of smell will often react very badly. An un-neutered Queen may no longer be interested in mating, many cats stop eating, others start marking and spraying indoors for the first time. We need to make sure our beloved pets do not suffer infections such as cat flu that can damage or destroy their sense of smell.

27

Count the Feet

And now for something a little different. In 'count the feet' you don't actually play interactively with your cat, but he takes part in your game, even if he doesn't know it. There are always disagreements in every household, even if they're only over trivia like 'whose turn is it to wash up' and 'you answer the phone this time – no, I did it last time' etc. There are various traditional ways of settling these minor disputes – such as playground games (stone, scissors, paper etc), making notes of job rotas so that disagreements don't arise, throwing temper tantrums, and even using violence.

There's another fair (and peaceful) method which has the added advantage that if you don't like the decision, you can blame the poor defenceless cat. To play, the cat has to be out of sight of both parties to the dispute, and each player has to guess how many of the cat's feet will be showing when they find him. So, John guesses two feet, but Anne thinks that no feet will be showing. When they find Ginger the cat, they discover that he is indeed curled up with all his feet tucked in, and so Anne wins. This leads to the obvious question – what if they're both wrong? Well, you could go by who's nearer – in this case, either three or four feet showing would have meant a win for John, who guessed two. But if only one foot had been showing, they would both have missed the correct answer by one, and any fair-minded referee would declare a draw and order them to share the disputed task. Another possibility for declaring a draw arises if they can't actually find the cat – this is a void result and it's not the cat's fault – he's doubtless got something better to do than deal with humans and their problems.

You could actually play this game merely to pass the time, or indeed money could change hands according to the result. Just small wagers are recommended or, after a run of heavy losses, you might begin to wonder if the game was rigged and the cat was being bribed.

My near neighbours John and Anne are retired now, and have a lot more time to themselves. They often go away for days out, or weekends away. Ginger isn't actually their cat, but he is well known in the neighbourhood and goes from house to house in the hope of finding someone at home who will take him in for a square meal and a good sleep on an armchair. When they're home, John and Anne look out for Ginger and, fingers crossed, he usually appears sometime during the morning. He actually lives a few houses down the street, but for some reason the attractions of other people's houses are stronger, and he's off on his rounds every morning. Rumour has it that he gets well fed by at least three households, though he has kept his figure well despite the feasting – I expect that he's out quite a lot at night working off the calories.

Getting back to the subject of counting the feet, Ginger is totally unpredictable. He is just as likely to be found completely curled up with all his feet tucked inside, or stretched out in a more dog-like posture with all his legs extended. I have heard that both John and Anne, if they have won today's 'count the feet' game with Ginger's help, have been known to secretly slip him an extra titbit – 'thanks for your help Ginger, it's three feet tomorrow, OK?'

– PB

"Three feet showing — you win."

30

"No feet showing —
better luck next time."

Hearing

Selective deafness aside (a lifelong condition that causes a cat to be unable to hear the word 'no' at whatever pitch it is spoken, while the slightest, quietest sound produced by tin-opening equipment provokes an instant response) a cat has wonderful hearing over a wide range of frequencies.

The lovely furry, responsive outer ear or 'pinna' acts like a megaphone in reverse, collecting sound, amplifying it and passing it on to the eardrum. The eardrum vibrates against three tiny bones, individually known as the hammer, anvil and stirrup, and collectively called ossicles, which in turn pass on the vibrations to the inner ear, known as the cochlea. This is filled with fluid and lined with tiny sensitive hairs which detect sounds and pass them on to the auditory nerve and thence to the part of the brain that interprets sound.

The system is basically the same as a human's – the most obvious difference is the cat's ability to swivel its pinna around to detect and locate sound. A cat will also use its ears to signal to others what it intends to do and how it is feeling. Generally speaking, a mammal with a smallish head and ears will hear higher sound frequencies, and a large head and ears are better for hearing lower frequencies.

Cats could be expected to have difficulty hearing lower, male human voices, but so exceptional is their hearing that they can hear the full range of human sounds. It may be that this is a major factor that has led to cats becoming domesticated. This ability to hear a sound and also to pinpoint where it comes from obviously helps a cat to hunt successfully, and it also increases their enjoyment of play. The satisfying crackle of paper, or the ping of a table-tennis ball when it is attacked, all add to the fun.

33

Mobiles

We have probably all seen mobiles. They have become a very popular type of ornament, especially in children's nurseries, where they serve as entertainment for infants as they lie in their cots and look up at the ceiling. Such mobiles are delicate structures and are balanced with almost watchmaker's precision. They rely for their movement on small currents of air, such as warm air gently rising, to make them move and rotate. Would this type be suitable for your cat? I don't think so. The life expectancy of this kind of mobile with a cat playing with it would probably be measured in seconds!

A cat mobile can be based on the same principles but needs to be constructed very robustly. Unlike a child's mobile, it need not be based on balanced bars with second and third tiers. A type of mobile which works well with a number of boisterous cats we know can be made quite easily.

Using a broom handle or a similar length of wood, tie loops of cord to the handle so that the attachment points are about a hand's width apart. The length of cord can vary to make loops of different lengths. Tie a toy at the bottom of each loop – any toy will do, including pieces of coloured ribbon or bows made of paper. You will now have a toy suspended from the broom handle on the end of each 'V' of cord. In this way, the toy can now swing, but in one plane of movement only.

Now set up the mobile – your cat may swing on it, so it needs to be firmly mounted. One end could be on a stair tread for example, with the other end across a kitchen stool. A pair of chairs also makes good supports. To start your cat playing with the mobile, show him what to do by setting one toy swinging back and forth. If your cat gets the idea quickly, start another toy swinging until all the toys on the mobile are in motion. They should swing to and fro at different speeds, which gives another visual stimulus.

A more sophisticated form of mobile can be made with two broom handles lashed together at right angles to each other. This, in effect, makes a double mobile with twice the number of toys suspended on it. This also has the advantage that the toys will swing in two planes of motion, not just one. If you tie one end of the loop to one broom handle and the other end to the other handle, the toy will swing at 45 degrees to the others, creating a complex pattern of moving shapes. This should all make the mobile very engaging for your cat, not to say irresistible.

Eventually, the mobile should become a standard part of your cat's life and will play the same sort of role for him that using a mini gym does for us. My friend Karen has an energetic cat called Oscar, who she thinks must have seen Lennox Lewis and Mike Tyson training on the speedball – you know, the ball suspended at about head height which swings back when you hit it. Like a boxer training, Oscar uses alternate paws to bat the toys on his mobile and gets them all swinging. He has learned to settle himself into a sitting position, which lets him use both front paws at once. Despite all this vigorous exercise, Oscar has recently been showing worrying signs of turning into a heavyweight. Now, boxing for cats – that sounds like a whole new book.

– PB

"This keeps me fighting fit — even if I do fall over sometimes."

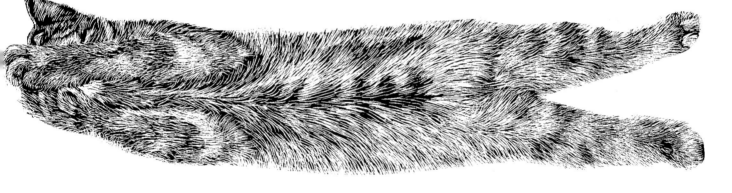

Happy Landings

A cat's ability to climb and balance is legendary, but even the most skilful exponent of the feline arts can sometimes make a mistake. Perhaps the twig was less strong than it looked, or the surface less rigid than expected, but whatever the cause, a fall is the regrettable outcome.

For a human this could be disastrous, but for a cat it's likely to be no more than a passing embarrassment. A straightforward drop fall is cushioned by the shock absorbers of the feet and shoulders. A cat's shoulders are held in place by powerful muscles, and not attached to large clavicles (collar bones) as are humans' shoulders. This makes cats much more flexible and capable of absorbing and dissipating huge forces such as those involved when landing from a great height. To take advantage of this wonderful system, and to avoid injury to the head and spine, if a cat is falling backwards or upside down it can quickly right itself and land feet first.

Before high-speed photography it was difficult to see exactly what happens, but we now know the sequence of events. As soon as the cat starts to fall, it twists its head round to see what it is falling onto. It then brings its paws in close to its body and twists around in mid-air. As soon as the cat is facing the right way, the legs are extended and the landing is completed successfully with only the cat's dignity affected.

All of this can be accomplished in an incredibly short time. A quick wash and brush up usually sorts everything out and our favourite feline is ready either to continue on his way, or perhaps to play a less dangerous game with his human companion – maybe something restful like 'Count the Feet'.

Egg Box

Many grocery stores sell eggs in boxes holding half a dozen each, and some have eggs on trays holding about two dozen. These moulded plastic or cardboard boxes and trays are extremely useful as cat toys and are usually available for nothing, or at least you get one free when you buy the eggs. The folding type of egg boxes can be cut apart to make smaller trays.

The first use of an egg tray is to make a version of a pin table for your cat. Use your thumbs to crush a line of the high points of the egg tray so that there is now a groove running along the tray. Using the same technique, make two or three other grooves running in different directions. You now need a ball that will fit in the grooves. Try propping up one end of the tray and rolling the ball down one of the grooves. Most cats will be intrigued by this and will show a fascination similar to their reaction to water flowing down plugholes.

You can change the angle of the tray while the ball is rolling to steer it along from one groove to another. Now it's your cat's turn. Place a ball at the start of a slope, just lodged in one of the egg recesses, and with the tray carefully angled so that, as soon as your cat disturbs it with his paw, it will roll down. Once he gets the hang of it, you could join in on vocals and make the game a multi-media experience by singing Pinball Wizard.

My cat Twirl enjoys this pinball game – she's now quite old but still loves to play. The beauty of playing pinball with her is that she can have all the fun of batting the ball and watching it roll without needing to be too energetic – or me too for that matter.

The next use of an egg box is the cat equivalent of a treasure hunt. Egg trays resemble the trays inside selection boxes of chocolates, with an individual recess for each chocolate. Using this principle, make a selection box of cat goodies. Cut the egg tray into a number of pieces, so that each piece has several recesses. Put a selection of cat treats into the egg spaces, but not too many if your cat's on a diet. Cover the treats and the empty egg spaces with table tennis balls or similar – large coins will do.

Hide the tray when you're next going out and your cat is staying in. The best places are behind furniture, in corners and so on, where they are not likely to get kicked over or trodden on. Your cat probably won't find the selection box every time. It is a fascinating test of your cat's curiosity and hunting skills to see how often he does find them, and how many (if any) he misses. It is also a test of the cat's ability to learn from experience and to use that experience to plan further searches. Just remember not to let your cat see you hiding them.

The egg box game can also be played as a simple 'find the titbit'. Place the tray on the floor with all the spaces covered over with balls, but with only some spaces containing a cat treat, and watch as your cat knocks the balls off, one at a time, hunting for the treat.

After all that work, you deserve a treat too – why not sit down with a selection box of chocolates.

– PB

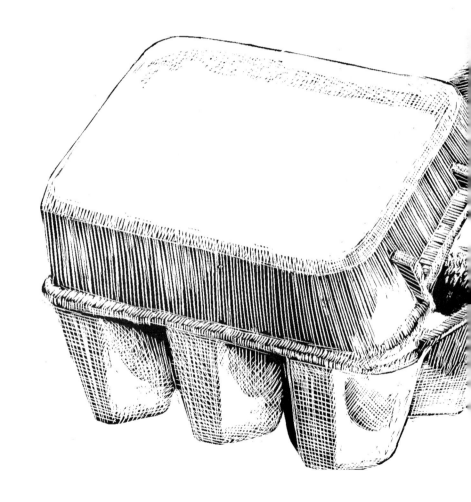

43

Food

The average weight of humans in the prosperous developed world is inexorably increasing. Given unrestricted access to food, many humans overeat to a frightening extent and, as a result, the proportion of obese people is increasing. Most cats, however, appear to be able to recognise high-calorie food and cut down their consumption. About 10% of cats, given the chance, will overeat, but the other 90% are very efficient at regulating their weight. The truly overweight cat, as opposed to one that is just naturally chubby, is a rare sight. Most cats, if they have eaten well at one meal, will cut down at the next.

An experiment was done to try to determine what eating pattern cats would establish if they were given constant access to food. On the whole, cat owners offer their pets two or three meals a day. Left to themselves though, the cats in the experiment ate up to twenty small meals in a twenty-four hour period. Oddly enough, although cats are nocturnal creatures, these cats took slightly bigger meals in the daytime than at night. So, for most cats, it is probably quite acceptable to leave some dried food out for your pet to snack at when he feels like it (don't forget to make some water available too).

Until relatively recently, virtually all cats had access to the great outdoors, but now with the increase in the number of flat dwellers, the proportion of cats who live totally indoors is increasing. Given the right care and diet, indoor cats can enjoy happy and healthy lives. To make sure that your indoor cat gets enough exercise, try to make time for active play every day, as an overweight cat who is out of condition will not be a happy purrer. Probably all of the proprietary cat foods, widely available from general stores and pet specialists, are of good quality and properly balanced to give the full range of nutrients that cats need. Some cats will develop a liking for one particular brand of food or type of treat above all others, and there is no harm in this, but most prefer a variety and we owners feel better serving up a mixed diet for our animal friends. For cats and humans alike, I think we can agree that a little of what you fancy does you good!

45

Waterball

Most people wrongly assume that all cats are naturally averse to water and to getting wet. While it is true that most cats don't readily jump into water as so many dogs will, there are many that nevertheless do show a great deal of interest in water. André's cat Emily is fascinated by the shower in his bedroom. Whenever he takes a shower, she is usually there to watch. She likes to perch on the side of the bath at the tap end, and watches with total fascination the soap suds going down the plug hole. She has even been known, on occasion, to jump in and paw at the suds.

Bearing this in mind, playing with your cat and water is not as odd as it might seem. For a simple game of cat ping-pong, use a shallow tray or a similar container. Place it on the floor and fill it to about two-thirds full with water. You'll also need a thin tube (such as a plastic drinking straw) and a few table-tennis balls. If you're playing indoors, it's best to put a plastic sheet under the tray to protect the floor.

Start the game by gently splashing the water with your fingers to attract your cat's attention. Next, put one of the balls on the water. To make it move in an interesting way, you'll need to use the tube to blow it across the water. With a bit of luck, your cat will now try pawing at the ball on the water and will bat it with his paw, making it move without your having to blow it. If you are very fortunate and have a super-intelligent cat, he may bat the ball in your direction and wait for you to return it.

A variation is to play with two or more balls. This can provide more visual stimulus for your cat and might help the more reluctant animals to join in and have fun.

There are a number of alternatives and additions to this general game which are worth trying. For example, following on what we said about André's cat Emily and the suds in the shower, why not put some washing-up liquid in the water and make it frothy? Whisk it with your fingers or blow bubbles with the straw. The froth creates a visual effect of 'icebergs' and can make for a more fascinating game. You can also try dropping the table-tennis ball into the water. Given that this type of ball weighs almost nothing, the splash is minimal, but the effect from a cat's perspective is very exciting. Yet more variation can be had by pouring the water into the tray from a jug at the start of the game. Cats are fascinated by sounds every bit as much as by other stimuli, and the sound of running and splashing water is very attractive to many of them.

Yet another version of this game uses dripping water. For this version, you'll need a jug to drip water slowly onto the surface of the water already in the tray. Vary the height of the jug above the tray – more height, more splash. The resulting splashing effect should make sufficient noise and ripples to intrigue your cat. With a steady hand, you'll soon develop the knack of aiming the dropping water so that it falls just behind the table-tennis ball and propels it across the water. If you've got several balls afloat, you can make them collide into each other.

After a few games, you and your cat will find endless ways of having fun with water .... and don't forget your shower!

– RM

47

48

*"I don't really mind
getting my paws
just a little bit wet"*.

Intelligence

Many cat owners will tell you that their pet knows every word they say, and will spend inordinate amounts of time relating the story of their favourite animal's perspicacity. Scientists, on the other hand, have often been dismissive of a cat's thinking and analysing ability. I believe this to be unfair as the cats used in intelligence experiments are often asked to learn complex tasks in unfamiliar, stressful situations. Unlike dogs, cats do not take easily to training by humans, but they can work things out for themselves. Many cats have taught themselves 'tricks' like opening doors, even ones with quite complex latches, as well as pressing switches, and finding complex routes that lead to food and comfort.

In the days before cat flaps, my grandmother had a huge ginger cat called Peter and he obviously noticed that, when people used the door knocker, grandma went to the door and let them in. He decided he could do the same. He stretched right up and lifted the knocker up then let it go. As he could lift it only a short way, grandma soon got to know his soft knock. One day she heard it when she was on top of a ladder and ignored it until, after a time, Peter's gentle knock was replaced by a loud human one. When she eventually got down from the ladder and opened the door she saw a smug Peter and a helpful passer-by who said, 'Hey missus, your cat wants to come in – you must have missed his knock'.

To be fair to scientists, they are now using cats in their normal habitats to come to conclusions about lifestyle and intelligence. It seems that, as in humans, the active, stimulated cat with access to toys and adventure will be brighter and more alert than a lazy, bored cat.

51

Shoebox

The shoebox and the many varied games you can play with it are very useful additions to your cat's toy library, and will give you both a tremendous amount of fun. The traditional type of shoebox is ideal, but other boxes of similar size, as long as they have lids, will do just as well.

Cut a hole about in the middle of the longer side, and just a little above the base of the box. This is so that, when you roll a ball to and fro inside the closed box, your cat will be able to see it pass the hole. Put the ball inside – a table-tennis ball, being light, cheap and noisy is ideal – and, if you wish, loop an elastic band around the box to stop the top coming off. Lift one end of the box off the floor to make the ball roll, then the other end so that it rolls back again. Your cat should first be attracted by the noise, and should then briefly glimpse the ball going past the hole.

After a few rolls back and forth, his curiosity should get the better of him and he'll want to look closely at the hole and the ball, and hopefully will try to get the ball with his paw. You can introduce variety by rocking the box along its short side, to make the ball go towards the hole and away again. Alternatively, you can make extra holes in the other sides of the box, so that as your cat circles the suspiciously noisy box with its mysterious ball inside, he keeps seeing the ball from different directions. As a reward for good playing, finally take off the lid and either let the cat get at the ball inside, or tip it out onto the floor for him to chase.

A different way to play Shoebox is to make a small hole in one of short ends of the box and thread a length of string through, tying it inside so that you can tow the box along the floor. If you jerk the box and vary the direction of pull, the ball will rattle about inside the box as it rolls. Your furry friend should enjoy the dual novelty of a box which moves by itself, and the exciting noise coming from inside it. Whichever way you play Shoebox, you can step up the noise and excitement by putting extra balls in the box, so that they knock into each other, as well as against the sides of the box.

Once he has got used to the magically moving box, you can develop the game by placing it on rollers (round pencils work well on a smooth wooden floor). Half a dozen carefully placed table-tennis balls also work well, and have the advantage that they let the box move freely for a short distance in any direction. This time, when he approaches the box and gives it a tentative bat with his paw to see what it's all about, the box will roll along the floor and the ball will move about inside the box. At first, he will probably be surprised by this amazing result – boxes don't usually take off by themselves when he prods at them – but he should find it intriguing and exciting.

As before, to round the game off, open the box and tip out the ball so that your cat can 'win' and get the ball.

– RM

"Where's that ball gone?
There it is again.
I'll get it next time."

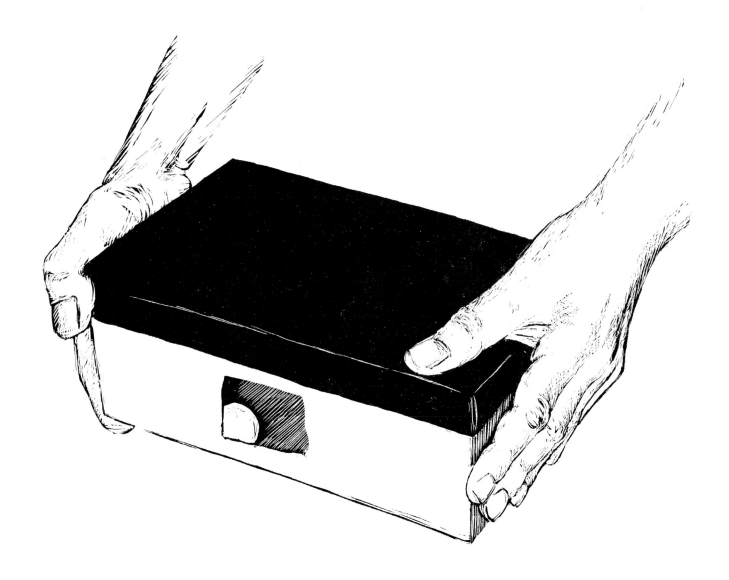

55

Teeth and Claws

Cats are carnivorous and are tremendously skilful hunters. To aid them in their quest for prey, they have highly flexible paws to make best use of their claws. Cats also have specialised dentition to help them deal with their catch once it has been secured. A cat cannot see things just in front of its face, but its flexible paws help to compensate for this as he can use them to hold objects in his field of vision. Normally, cats keep their claws retracted – when they play they usually keep their claws out of the way. When the need arises however, these claws can flash out and be ready for action in a fraction of a second. The claws are not only very sharp, but also curve backward to improve the cat's grip and to help them to position their prey effectively. These useful weapons also facilitate a cat's climbing activities, giving them wonderful grip. A cat scrabbling up a fence will support his weight with his paws as he drags himself to the top.

Claws need to be kept sharp and at the right length – scratching against a rough surface such as a tree (or, more likely, your best furniture) does the trick nicely. Indoor cats with a low activity level may need to have their claws trimmed from time to time, but this should only be done by people who really know what they're doing.

Cats' teeth are very different from the human variety. If your favourite cat will let you, look at his teeth and you will see that the front teeth (incisors) are very small compared with the other teeth. The incisors are used primarily in grooming and to do some light nibbling work. Next to them are the killer teeth, the canines. These are long, sharp and sensitive to pressure, and are what a cat uses to kill its prey by biting between the vertebrae of the neck. A cat's set of teeth includes premolars and molars but, unlike humans with their flat-topped teeth for grinding food, a cat's molars are designed to slice through food. Generally, rough playing where the cat uses his teeth and claws to attack your fingers is best discouraged because, if he forgets for a moment that it's only a game, your cat can easily sink his teeth right through to the bone and you'll have to be very forgiving to keep smiling.

57

Fishing Line – Version 2

Fishing line games can also be played in a 'ground target' based way. In this type of game you are trying to simulate the type of prey, other than birds, your cat would naturally hunt. To play this kind of game, you'll need one or two other items, such as a light rug or cloth to place on the floor and some light boxes.

'Round the corner' games are often favourites. Find your cat – if he's inside the room, place the toy on the end of the fishing line on the floor just inside the doorway, on the same side of the door as the cat. Stand outside the doorway so that your cat cannot see you. Start to jerk on the line so that you make the toy move in very small but jerky movements to attract your cat's attention. If you are using a toy mouse or a ball, it will help if it's the type with a bell inside which jingles as it moves.

Your cat will, with a bit of luck, go into 'stalking' mode, going down on his haunches and approaching the target as slowly and carefully as he can without being detected. Just before pouncing, he will tend to wiggle his bottom slightly as he gears up for an explosive burst of energy to propel himself at the target with ferocious determination. It's when you watch fascinating moments like this that you realise what superb and magnificent creatures cats are, and what supremely good hunters they have become. It also makes you realise how deadly the big cats – lions, tigers and so on – are when they need to hunt to survive.

Another great game to play is 'Under the Rug'. In this game the target toy is placed under a rug or cloth on the floor. It is then a matter of pulling on the line with short jerking movements to attract the cat's attention. Eventually, after much pouncing and attacking, pull the target toy out from under the rug so that your cat can have the satisfaction of the final kill. More intrepid cats will burrow under the rug to get at the target and will follow the toy under the rug, emerging again into the daylight as you pull the toy out from under. My cat Cleo is not usually very brave, but she likes to burrow, particularly under the bedclothes on cold nights, and plays the 'Under the Rug' game enthusiastically.

Boxes can provide yet more fun. For this game, you need a medium-sized cardboard box. What you do is cut a 'mousehole' in the side of the box just big enough for the toy attached to the line to be pulled out of the box. The hole will also let your cat push his paw into the box to try to retrieve the toy. Place the box, open side down, on the floor. Jerk the line to make toy move and make a noise inside the box. Your cat probably won't turn the box over or burrow underneath it, but will biff the side of it, making it slide about, and look into the mousehole. He may also try to get a paw inside the mousehole to get at the toy inside. Your job is to keep the cat's attention by jerking on the line, keeping the movement and noise going. Eventually, let your cat 'win' by pulling the toy clear of the hole on the side of the box so that he can give it the coup de grâce.

– RM

"That pesky mouse can run — but it can't hide from me."

61

Running, jumping and standing still

Mention cats and adjectives such as 'elegant' and 'graceful' spring to mind. The beauty of their movements is, in my opinion, unsurpassed in the animal kingdom.

Cats walk on their toes and their footbones are elongated to facilitate running at speed. A cat's leg joints, while they are virtually the same as human joints in their type of movement, are arranged differently in relation to the cat's body. The cat's knee, for instance, is much closer to the body. If you look at a photograph of a cat in motion, you can see which joint is which from the way it bends. Another significant difference between the way the cat is put together and human-type construction is in the shoulders. The cat's shoulder blades are lined up on the side of the body, held in position by thick bands of muscles. This arrangement helps the cat produce its characteristic walk, with one paw directly behind the other.

Proportionately, more weight is carried by the forepaws when the cat is walking, and the powerful muscles in the hindquarters and back provide the 'push'. The cat's vertebrae are more loosely articulated than a human's, again helping to give the cat its litheness. If it has a firm place to leap from, a cat can jump several times its own length either upwards or downwards.

The part of the leg in touch with the ground — the paw — and in particular the pads, also play their part in reducing the impact of movement on the cat's skeleton. Paws and pads provide a significant amount of shock absorption when a cat jumps. The skin on the surface of the pads is very special, being up to 70 times as thick as normal epithelial tissue (skin). A cat will pay particular attention to looking after its paws, as damaged pads can be both painful and disabling. The only problem with paws is that most cats don't like having their paws touched, which is a shame because pads and paws are attractive and are just asking to be played with. It's worth a try, as some cats are more considerate and will let you play with their feet. They probably think that they are playing with you. I have heard a rumour that a group of cats are getting together to produce a book called 'Games To Play With Your Human' — I wonder where they got the idea from?

63

Spinner Winner

Ever thought you could be a successful gambler if only you could beat the huge odds stacked against you? Answer – get the cat to help. This game finds winning (well, maybe) numbers for lotteries, football pools, roulette etc.

To make a Spinner Winner, cut a circle and an arrow out of cardboard. Find the centre of the arrow by balancing it on the point of the scissors, then push the scissors through. Make a spacer out of cardboard to go between the circle and the arrow – this will help the arrow to spin without dragging. To mark out the circle, ideally use a protractor and mark out angles of 36° (any school child will help you with this). If you've got a dart board, follow the markings on the board and just use every other one to give ten segments. Failing this, cut ten small strips of card and arrange them around the edge of the circle until they're evenly spaced, then ink them in. For the spindle, use a wire bag-tie doubled over – line up the holes in the circle, the spacer and the arrow and push it through. Spread out the ends of the bag tie on the underside of the circle.

There are two ways of playing this game. More adventurous cats will follow your example and bat the arrow with their paws – note down the number where it stops. Other cats will watch you spin the arrow, then pounce on it – again, note where it stops. **Important note** – this game is not guaranteed to give you winning numbers, but if your furry friend does actually choose the numbers that win you millions, the least you can do is share your good fortune – a nice piece of salmon would be very acceptable.

My friend Danielle plays Spinner Winner with her cats Poppy and Grace. They have very different personalities – Poppy is quite timid with people she doesn't know well, but she's affectionate with her friends and very vocal. Grace likes to remain aloof and pretend that she has grown out of kittenish behaviour. When the Spinner Winner board comes out, Poppy starts to get excited and yowls happily, but Grace stays curled up on her favourite comfortable chair and pretends to go to sleep, but if you look closely you'll see that she's usually got at least one eye partly open.

Poppy likes Spinner Winner – the first few times she played the game she started off by watching the spinning pointer for a second or two before pouncing, but then she got bolder, and now she likes to spin the pointer herself and watch it as it slows down to a halt. Danielle suspects that Poppy secretly thinks the Spinner Winner board is alive, because once the pointer has come to a halt, she is very wary about approaching it again for a few seconds. She crouches and watches the pointer like a lion waiting to strike, then, when she's sure there's no danger, she bats the pointer again and watches it spin.

Danielle has never actually seen Grace playing Spinner Winner, but one day when the game was on the sitting room floor and Poppy was asleep upstairs, Danielle came back into the room and saw the pointer just coming to a halt. Grace, who'd heard Danielle coming, was sitting a short distance away washing herself and looking slightly flustered, not to say guilty. There's never been any evidence of paranormal activity in Danielle's household, so you can draw your own conclusions.

– PB

"If I come up
with the right
numbers,
it'll be best
salmon for me
every day."

The Kitten Cat

New-born kittens, up to the age of about three weeks, are very dependent on their mothers and are too busy eating and sleeping to explore the play potential of the world – but that soon changes!

At three to four weeks old, kittens are starting to look very cute indeed. Their legs are strong enough to support their bodies off the floor, though they are not quite 100% upright. Their ears are properly upright and mostly under control, as are their tails. Until this stage, a kitten is not usually able to hold its little taper tail up straight, but now it can, and this, combined with much clearer-looking eyes, gives the quintessential kitten 'look' so beloved of calendar manufacturers. Once a kitten can focus properly and has control of its limbs and senses, it can start to learn to play. Five-week-old kittens turn almost overnight into playing machines. They love to pounce and climb – the legs of a friendly human sitting nearby are often selected as a suitable climbing frame.

All their faculties and equipment will now be tried out, including their teeth. They will gnaw on almost everything including any fingers left incautiously lying around. This vigorous playing soon tires tiny kittens and exhaustion will suddenly overcome them, leading to the need for frequent catnaps.

At six weeks, kittens can play with whatever is to hand. If a mother cat were living wild, she would bring prey home and her kittens would grip it and fight for possession of it. In the absence of this stimulus, we humans can provide similar stimulation with toys as you'll see in the rest of this book.

One plaything that doesn't need to be simulated (except perhaps with a litter of Manx kittens) is the tail. Kittens find their mother's gently-moving tail irresistible, as are the more rapidly-moving tails of their siblings. Little kittens are also very interested in their own tails but never quite catch them.

Kittens move on to solid food at around seven weeks old, and can go to their new homes at around eight weeks, having learned all the basic skills they need – usually including litter training – from their mother, her humans and their litter mates. Ten-week-old kittens have more or less the posture and characteristics of adults. They still play vigorously and dart about in a kittenish way, and because a loved house cat doesn't really have to adopt adult behaviour and become the mighty hunter in order to survive, many cats retain their youthful playful natures all their lives.

Feathers

Cats seem to be naturally attracted to feathers and will readily play with them. This might have something to do with their tendency to hunt birds. The first thing to do, if you want to have some fun with your cat playing with feathers, is to decide what type of feathers to use. Handfuls of small feathers can be good, but they can lead to a bit of a mess. If, however, you want to use this type of feather, an old feather pillow is ideal. Nowadays, the majority of pillows are filled with 'hollow fibre' and an old pillow of this type will yield plenty of suitable feather substitute. New pillows filled with hollow fibre are very cheap anyway, and if you only use a small amount, the remainder can be recycled as a new mattress for your cat. If you want to play with a few large feathers, you can often find them lying around in the countryside or in the garden.

There are lots of games that can be played with feathers. My cat Cleo loves to play what I call 'flying feather'. This involves me dropping a few small feathers from my upstairs landing down to the hallway. Cleo loves to dart about, going from one feather to the other as she hunts them. I can see her using all of her strongest hunting instincts when we play this game, lying in wait, crouching and pouncing. The game can be extended by blowing the feathers to keep them up in the air for longer. A piece of cardboard in the shape of an old-fashioned fan works well to create breezes which keep the feathers in the air. If your cat doesn't mind the noise, using a vacuum cleaner set on 'blow' makes an exciting variation on the game.

That good old favourite, the cardboard tube, comes in handy for another version of the feathers game. Place a feather in the tube, get down on the floor to get your cat's attention, then blow the feather out of the tube up into the air. As before, using a few feathers will make the game more interesting when they flutter in all directions. You can also use the tube to direct a jet of air at the feathers to keep them afloat for longer.

There was a slightly embarrassing outcome of the feathers game one day. Cleo and I had been playing a particularly energetic game, running around the whole ground floor of my house, and I had not yet cleaned up afterwards (typical man). I had invited a new friend round and I'd put out a tray with cups, milk, sugar and biscuits. She came a bit earlier than expected and we sat down for a chat while the kettle was boiling. When I came to pour out the coffee, we both noticed that there were small bits of feathers in the milk jug and in the cups, not to mention on the biscuits. Cleo had gone upstairs for a sleep, tired and happy after the game, and I didn't really think I could blame her for doing something awful when I was the one who had started the game. Alternatively, I could own up to having played the feathers game with Cleo and to being a bit lax on the housework front. I decided that honesty was the best policy and shouldered the blame. The social occasion passed pleasantly, but I did notice that my friend inspected her cup, biscuit, milk, and lump of sugar carefully but discreetly in case there were any feathers (or worse) waiting to be consumed.

– RM

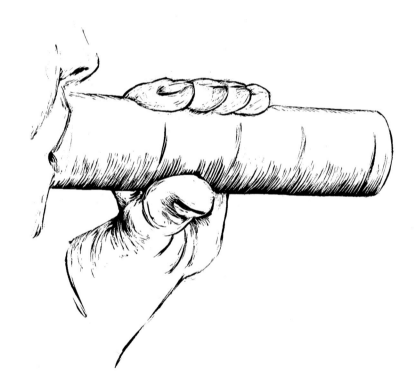

73

Heads and Tails

The most skilful highwire act known to man is no match for the average family cat when it comes to balance and grace. The organ that controls balance in both humans and felines is the vestibular system, located inside the skull. There are three semicircular canals arranged more or less at right angles to each other. These canals are filled with fluid and lined with sensitive cells which detect movement of the fluid. Each of the fluid-filled semicircles registers the cat's position in space. The angles at which they are set and the accuracy of their positional detection enable the cat to move easily on narrow fences and branches. They also find it easy to leap onto narrow, high ledges or onto the tops of thin poles and instantly balance.

The accuracy of their balancing and positioning is legendary. The young Twirl got her name from her ability to throw herself high into the air, twisting as she went, catch a fly and then land absolutely accurately in the centre of the most precious plant that had just that day, after months of careful nurturing, reached full blooming perfection.

Apart from the tailless Manx cat, a tail also helps the cat to balance, particularly when climbing trees. A tail can help a fast-moving cat that needs to change direction quickly, by acting as a counterbalance. A cat that has had its tail amputated due to disease or accident may take some time to adjust his behaviour to take account of the changed circumstances. One cat, Peter, a handsome black neutered male, was obviously very self conscious after losing most of his tail following an argument with a car – so much so that he spent several days in the guinea pigs' cage. The guinea pigs kindly shared their space with him while he made the necessary psychological and physical adjustments.

The psychological aspect of the tail is important as a cat uses the tail to signal mood and intent. The 'bottle brush' effect produced when a cat is either fearful or aggressive makes him look bigger and more impressive. The way in which a tail is moved will give onlookers a good idea if a cat is angrily swishing it or idly twitching it. A cat happily trotting along with his tail held high is a sight to gladden any cat lover's heart

75

Rope Snake

Wave motion is one of those topics which either fascinated us in school physics lessons, or bored us rigid. Whatever your level of knowledge of theoretical physics, don't worry, this game won't even mention lambda or sinusoidal wave motion. However, dear reader, you are familiar with what happens when you wiggle a length of cord or rope. A wave pattern flows down the cord to the other end. You can wiggle up and down, or side to side, the wave pattern is much the same. It doesn't matter how hard or gently you do it, the speed of the waves along the rope is about the same, only the wavelength (the distance between successive peaks or troughs) and the amplitude (the height of the waves) vary. Is this the point in school when you started looking out of the window and dreamed of being a pop singer or a footballer?

All this super science can be harnessed to the task in hand, having lots of fun with your cat. To make a Rope Snake, all you need is a length of rope or cord. Start by simply wiggling the rope to make waves along its length. This alone should be enough to make your cat come running to investigate what the new toy is. My neighbour's cat Ruffles loves to pounce on the end of the Rope Snake. To make an even more attractive snake, why not colour the rope with marker pens. Ideally, alternate black and white sections will make the snake extremely eye-catching to any cat.

Try taking the snake for a 'walk' by continuing to make waves while you walk along. This should be even more intriguing for your cat. The next development is to attach different toys along the length of the snake. The toys should be quite light so as not to upset the flowing wave motion too much – Ruffles' favourites are bows made of coloured ribbon, strips of coloured paper and jingly bells of the type that some cats have attached to their collars. Ruffles is an old cat now and sleeps most of the time, but the Rope Snake is one of the toys which will still get him out of his basket for a bit of fun and exercise.

There are numerous variations on the Rope Snake game. One such involves making a double snake. To make this, all you need is a short strip of wood. Tie a Rope Snake to each end of the strip and hold the strip in the middle, and then you will be able to set up a double wave pattern. Twice the fun! You can make the two snakes wiggle side by side like synchronised dancers, or you can rotate the strip of wood at the same time to make the snakes twist together while the waves are still running along their length.

Yet another version of the game is played by standing on a chair or kitchen step ladder and wiggling the rope vertically. While you're wiggling to make the waves, you can introduce a circular motion of your hand, which makes the pattern of waves even more varied. You can give the snake a brief siesta by letting it rest on the floor and then, just when your cat thinks the game's over and the snake can be safely investigated and sniffed at, you can wake it up again with a vigorous flick.

Rope Snake is such a fascinating yet simple way of having terrific fun with your cat, and you don't even have to have heard of Schrödinger's paradoxical cat to play it.

– *PB*

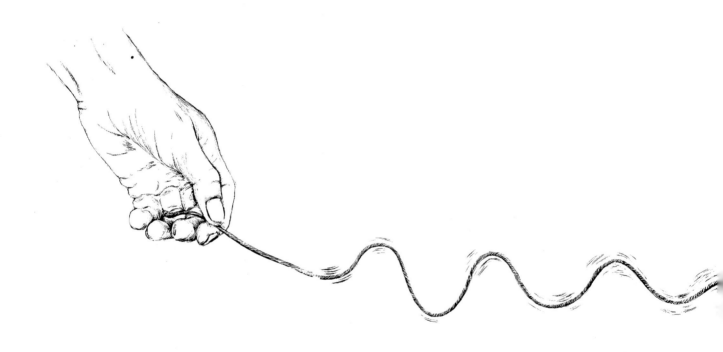

78

"I'm not sure
if it's a real snake
— but I'll catch it anyway."

Catnip

Only about half of all cats react to catnip, but those that do, react in a most immoderate way. If you have ever tried to grow catnip (Latin name Nepeta cataria) you will probably have had the same difficulty that I've had — namely, plants that have been bitten, chewed, rolled on, flattened and generally destroyed by the local cat population. It is said that growing the plants from seed is more successful than transplanting living plants because you do not have to handle and damage the plant itself to the same degree, and less of the aromatic oils produced by the plant are released into the air to attract passing felines.

The oils are secreted by both the stems and the leaves of the plant, and they affect some big cats, including lions, as well as domestic cats. The stately tiger appears immune to the charms of catnip, but lions become positively kittenish when playing in a patch of catnip. Cats affected by catnip are driven wild, rubbing their faces and rolling their bodies in it. They certainly seem to enter an altered state of consciousness and to enjoy getting high from the taste and scent. If you have a cat who has inherited the ability to detect the smell and you want to grow the plant, it is possible to buy dried catnip and to grow a less attractive version of the plant such as Nepeta mussinii. Dried catnip sprinkled on a man-made mouse or other furry toy hugely increases its attractiveness. Luckily, it quickly loses its potency on exposure to air, and the cat soon calms down.

One word of warning — don't try to take the catnip away from a cat until he loses interest in it. Even a cat not known for scratching may lash out under those circumstances!

Love and peace, man.

81

Stairball

All you need for this game is a flight of stairs, and a ball (oh yes, and a cat). There are lots of variations on the game. The basic game involves throwing the ball onto the stairs so that it rolls down again, one step at a time. Some cats will chase the ball up the stairs, but others will watch it as it rolls down, and finally catch it at the bottom of the stairs. If your cat is already upstairs, the sound of the ball bouncing down the stairs will often catch his curiosity and he will come to the top of the stairs. As an alternative to a ball, a cork works well because it does not roll evenly. Corks work better if you stand at the top of the stairs and throw them down.

Another good toy is a ball made of silver paper. Screwed-up paper balls work better the bigger they are – smaller ones don't seem to have as much bounce and often just stop wherever they land. My late lamented cat, Biggles, particularly liked paper balls because he could rip them up once he had caught them, but more polite cats will chase paper balls around the floor once they have landed at the bottom of the stairs

You can develop the game by throwing two balls together, or, if you have banister rails, throwing the ball or cork onto the stairs from the side. This adds another element to the game because you can pretend to throw the ball or cork from different positions so that your cat has got to watch exactly where your hand is to see whereabouts on the stairs the ball is going to come from.

My friend Jenny's cat Tilly (officially called Matilda) who is playing stairball in our picture, is a truly remarkable animal. As a kitten she always had very large ears, and then kept growing into them, and growing, and growing. We noticed that her ears were very warm to the touch, and when we investigated other cats' ears, we never found another cat with anything like the same warmth. It was obvious then that there was something out of the ordinary about Tilly. Although Tilly eats just a normal amount, she has weighed a steady 10kg for a few years now. When Jenny takes Tilly for a routine check up or for her annual injection, the staff all welcome her and ask how the famous Matilda is keeping before ceremoniously putting her on the scales. She has been the heaviest cat at the local animal health clinic for some years now. Tilly isn't the most active cat in the world – her usual place is lying upstairs in a drawer, keeping half an eye on the world, but when she does decide to run, the floor shakes!

Her companion is Topaz, whom Jenny took in as a stray. Topaz had lived outside for some years, but always stayed friendly and interested in people. When Jenny moved house, Topaz and Tilly moved with her. Tilly settled immediately as she had always lived indoors and her familiar food tray and favourite chair moved with her. Topaz surprised everyone by adapting straight away to indoor living. The first occasion she went out into the garden was a worrying time – we thought she might try to find her old home, but in fact she came back in again very quickly. Although she likes to be outside, she never roams far, often sitting on top of the garden shed for a panoramic view.

– PB

84

"I'll chase it down the stairs and catch it before it reaches the bottom."

Just Purrfect

One of the best situations you, as a cat lover, can enjoy is sitting in a warm room, on a comfortable chair, with your pet cat ensconced on your knee and purring like a bandsaw. What more telling picture of total contentment could there be? Cats do not just purr for their human companions. They start purring as kittens when drinking their mother's milk – mother, of course, is also purring.

The slightly older adolescent cat will also use purring when approaching an adult cat, and the adult will purr back to reassure the youngster. Our domestic cat is not alone in purring. All the cat's close relatives purr, including the hyena which, although doglike, is more closely related to the cat. Mongooses, civets and genets also purr when suckling their young. The purr that the mighty tiger produces when it exhales is something worth hearing!

The exact mechanism by which the cat produces its continuous purr is not quite clear. The ventricular chords (false vocal chords) in the throat seem to be involved. We also have not worked out why other mammals do not purr while suckling their young, or otherwise experiencing extreme contentment. The purr is an effective control and location mechanism. It is loud enough for kittens to keep contact with their litter mates, but not so loud that a passing predator would hear it. A mother cat's purr calms and reassures her kittens and ensures that they stay quiet and safe.

Some cats hardly purr at all. I had one special friend called Becket who vibrated gently but produced no sounds audible to my inadequate human ears. Conversely, all through her life Twirl has purred with varying degrees of volume. She walks around the house purring, in much the same way that some cheery souls hum, whistle and sing their way through life.

87

Wool

Balls of knitting wool are marvellous cat toys, and as such have been popular for a long time. The softness of the wool seems to be especially attractive to cats and, although it is quite strong in tension, wool is very easily shredded by a cat's claws with no danger that the claws will get caught or damaged. You can buy balls of wool in various sizes easily and cheaply in craft shops everywhere.

There are numerous games to play with balls of wool which are very popular with many cats we know. They can be used as toys on the end of the 'fishing line' games in this book. Their natural bounciness adds an extra fun dimension to fishing games – you can even make the ball bounce off your cat himself, without any danger of injury. Balls of wool can also be used as free-standing toy balls as part of your cat's toy library. In addition however, there are some other games which are very rewarding and well worth trying.

One of these is 'Find the Ball'. First tie one end of the wool to a suitable anchor point such as a door handle or chair leg. Next, pay out the wool as you take the ball to a suitable hiding place. This can be under a shoebox, behind a cushion or just about anywhere. Attract your cat's attention and show him the end of the wool that is tied to the anchor point. Make a circle with your finger and thumb around the wool and run it down the thread as you trace it along to the hidden ball. Hopefully, your cat will follow you, even if he is slightly bemused. 'Find' the ball and give it to your cat to play with. When you have done this a few times, your cat should have learned what the game is about and will trace the wool along its length without prompting to find the ball.

As a more advanced version of this game, set up a 'wool thread' trail as above, but this time, where the first thread ends and the cat finds the ball of wool, there is a second trail leading to a second ball of wool. You could add a third trail and so on – the limiting factor is probably the size of your home. You can also play this game outside, with the wool running behind trees and underneath plants, as well as round the garden furniture.

'Pull the Wool' is another fun game. Tie two balls of wool together using wool from the balls themselves, making sure that the wool is tied into the ball at both ends and the balls of wool will not unravel. There needs to be enough length of wool in between the balls for the balls to hang over a door handle with both balls hanging about halfway down from the handle to the floor. Show your cat the two balls of wool. He should be familiar with balls of wool by now and recognise them as playthings. Pull down on one ball so that the other one goes up, and vice versa. Knock one ball so that the two swing and bounce about. Your cat should be so intrigued by this that he will start to jump up at the balls, and in doing so will pull one down and one up. Eventually, it is in the nature of things that your cat will end up shredding the balls of wool, but that's what this game is really all about.

– PB

"Funny
— every time
I pull
one down,
the other one
goes up."

91

Settling in

By nature, the cat is a solitary hunter patrolling its own territory to keep it safe from interlopers, and also venturing out further into its home range around its own territory, to keep an eye on the rest of the world. Cats have, through the ages, been characterised as aloof and independent, but as we know they can be the most friendly and affectionate of companions. Like most of us humans when we were babies, our new cats are treated as babies and this sets the tone for their outlook on life. A cat's basic personality will not usually change but a cat that has been well fed and trained by its mum, and then goes to a loving and playful home, has a good start in life and is likely to make a wonderful happy pet.

Cats who live together, although this is not usually how they would choose to live in the wild, will often be affectionate to each other and even sleep huddled together and indulge in mutual grooming. This is most likely to be the case with cats that have grown up together. It can be difficult when cats are adopted as adults, although nine times out of ten the cats will adjust and settle down. A dear friend has two cats, one of which was adopted at a few months old, and the other was an adult stray. Unfortunately, these cats do not get on at all. One lives upstairs and the other down. Every so often, each one apparently decides that the other has the best of it, and they swap territories.

It is probable that we can keep several cats together successfully and harmoniously, somewhat contrary to what would happen in nature, because we make sure that food and comfort are readily available in quantity. Often a stray cat chooses the humans he wants to be with, but if you are picking a kitten, do look for signs of the basic personality. An outgoing, rough and tumble, loving type may suit you, or you may prefer a more self-contained observer of the human condition.

The cat and the human, though ostensibly so different in their approach to life, can live together very comfortably. I think the fact that we both like to be warm and well fed, and to sleep a lot, may have something to do with it.

93

Adventure Playground

An adventure playground for your cat serves the same function as a leisure centre does for humans. In other words, it is a self-contained complete focus for entertainment, leisure, exercise and relaxation. This makes a cat adventure playground ideal for cats who stay indoors but still like to be active. Likewise, if you are out for long periods, your cat can keep himself amused, entertained and healthy while you are out by exploring his playground environment. All the requirements for your pet should be catered for. The playground will probably be largely a combination of many of the toys and games so far discussed in this book. In addition, you have to provide some other items, including a bed or cushion for your cat to sleep on when he's feeling like a catnap, assuming he doesn't already sleep on your bed. There will also be his litter tray, a supply of food and water, and his scratching post if he uses one.

The layout of the adventure playground can be with everything close together, or it can be spread out around your home. For example, there can be mobiles in different rooms so that your cat will go from one room to another and find something new to play with. One layout we know of has a water tray with table tennis balls, followed by a mobile and then a couple of open shoeboxes with toys inside. You can also hide games in odd corners or behind pieces of furniture so that your cat literally has to go hunting for them. You can add further to the fun by hiding titbits among the games for your cat to find.

One section of the playground can include a cat's mini gym, designed specifically for exercising your cat. There is little or no cost involved. Set up a series of jumps by positioning several chairs or stools of different heights close enough together for the cat to be able to jump comfortably from one to the next. When they decide it's time for a rest (and that's quite a lot of the time) many cats love to crawl under soft warm coverings such as duvet covers on beds. When my cat Twirl does this she usually leaves just the end of her tail sticking out which makes her easy to find. You can include 'nests' in the playground by cutting up an old blanket into several pieces and placing these on chairs and in other cosy places where your cat likes to lounge. I find that pieces of blanket are more attractive to cats if they are crumpled up rather than laid flat. Cats also like the sounds coming from radios and televisions. You can leave a radio playing for just this purpose, and also to make your home sound occupied when you are out.

There is an infinite variety of arrangements and possibilities. Starting with the suggestions here, you will soon create your cat's own personal adventure playground/leisure centre.

Well, that's about it. We hope you've enjoyed reading our book as much as we enjoyed working out all the games and writing it. Our own cats and our friends' pets have given us all a great deal of pleasure over the years. We sincerely hope that this book can add to the pleasure you get from your cat. Please email us at paul_berman@yahoo.com or roger.markman@virgin.net with any suggestions for games that you may have, or feedback on how you've got on with the games we've sketched out here.

Good luck and happy games from both of us.

– PB & RM

And goodbye . . .

... from all of us!

Also from Sigma Leisure:

Walking & cycling guidebooks for the most scenic parts of England & Wales, featuring "Walks with Children", "Pub Walks", "Tea Shop Walks" and "Church Walks"

Adventure & Travel books – inspirational titles that include "The Bluebird Years: Donald Campbell & The Pursuit of Speed", "Himalaya Venture" and "Lonesome Rhodes: One Man, Two Wheels & 19,000 Miles"

Overseas walking guides for The Loire Valley, Brittany, Normandy, The Dordogne, The Alpujarra, Costa del Sol, Mallorca and Tuscany

Heritage and Local Interest – town and county guides, folklore, and recollections of bygone eras. Plus our classic "In Search of Swallows & Amazons"

All of our books are available through booksellers. In case of difficulty, or for a free catalogue, please contact:

SIGMA LEISURE, 1 SOUTH OAK LANE, WILMSLOW, CHESHIRE SK9 6AR.
Phone: 01625-531035 Fax: 01625-536800.   E-mail: info@sigmapress.co.uk
Web site: http//www.sigmapress.co.uk